CH

ID0793339

WHAT ARE LIVING & NONLIVING THINGS?

LOUISE SPILSBURY

Britannica®
Educational Publishing

IN ASSOCIATION WITH

ROSEN
EDUCATIONAL SERVICES

Published in 2014 by Britannica Educational Publishing (a trademark of Encyclopædia Britannica, Inc.) in association with The Rosen Publishing Group, Inc.
29 East 21st Street, New York, NY 10010

Distributed exclusively by Rosen Publishing.
To see additional Britannica Educational Publishing titles, go to rosenpublishing.com

First Edition

Britannica Educational Publishing
J.E. Luebering: Director, Core Reference Group
Anthony L. Green: Editor, Compton's by Britannica

Rosen Publishing
Hope Lourie Killcoyne: Executive Editor
Nelson Sá: Art Director

Library of Congress Cataloging-in-Publication Data

Spilsbury, Louise, author.
What are living & nonliving things? / Louise Spilsbury. — First edition.
    pages cm. — (Let's find out. Life science)
Includes bibliographical references and index.
ISBN 978-1-62275-226-3 (library binding) — ISBN 978-1-62275-229-4 (pbk.) — ISBN 978-1-62275-230-0 (6-pack)
1. Organisms—Juvenile literature. 2. Life (Biology)—Juvenile literature. I. Title.
QH309.2.S65 2014
570—dc23

2013023140

Manufactured in the United States of America.

Photo credits
Cover: Shutterstock: FikMik fg, Yuriy Kulik bg. Inside: Dreamstime: 7horses 18, Algul 22, BCritchley 12, Bobsphotography 9, Cathykeifer 11, Fouroaks 15, Hipgnosis 20, Intoit 14, Irfannurd 16, Ivonnewierink 26, Kateleigh 17, Kikkerdirk 13, Mangroove 28, Mishatc 19, Mitch1921 24, Mopic 25r, Nemul 5, Okea 10, Phildate 6, Pictureperfect79 23, Smartcoder 27, Stockshooter 7, Vitocork 8, Wickedgood 29, Zhekos 21; Shutterstock: FikMik 1fg, Mandy Godbehear 4, Yuriy Kulik 1bg, KV4000 25cl, Kati Molin 25cr, Valerie Potapova 25l.

CONTENTS

ALL AROUND US

Imagine walking down a busy street. You might see many living things, such as people, dogs, plants, insects, and birds. You might also see nonliving things, such as the sidewalk, buildings, and maybe puddles of water. Unlike nonliving things, living things need food and water to live.

People are living things.

Sometimes it can be difficult to tell the difference between living and nonliving things. For example, living things can move, but so can some nonliving things, such as cars and waves. Rocks are not alive, but some rocks, called crystals, grow like living plants. How do we know if something is alive or not?

THINK ABOUT IT
Make a list of the living and nonliving things in your home or school. Can you find any nonliving things made from living things?

The world around us is full of living and nonliving things.

LIVING THINGS

A little worm, a massive whale, the mightiest tree, and a tiny buttercup flower all look completely different. We can tell they are living things because they all carry out seven life processes. These are special abilities that allow living things to survive. All living things are able to carry out all of these life processes.

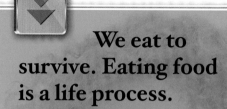

We eat to survive. Eating food is a life process.

Life processes are activities that living things must do to live.

This unusual desert plant looks like rock, but we know it is alive because it carries out all of the seven life processes.

You can remember the life processes by taking the first letter of each word to make the name, "Mrs. Nerg:"

Movement: the act of moving

Reproduction: ability to produce young

Senses: parts that respond and react

Nutrition: taking in and making use of food

Excretion: getting rid of waste

Respiration: turning oxygen into energy

Growth: getting to adult size

MOVEMENT

All living things can move. People and animals move to get food, to find partners with whom to have young, and to escape danger. Living things move in different ways.

Plants usually stay in one place, but they move as they grow and become taller. Many plants have leaves and flowers that move and turn to catch the sunlight.

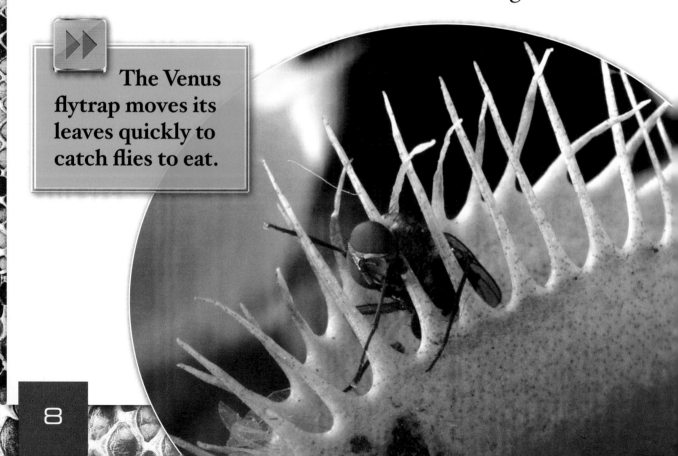

The Venus flytrap moves its leaves quickly to catch flies to eat.

A cheetah's long, strong legs help it run very fast!

COMPARE AND CONTRAST
Fish and birds move in different ways. Which body parts do they use to make them move, and how do they move them?

Animals have body parts that help them move in different ways. Monkeys have long arms and fingers so they can swing between branches in a forest. Whales and dolphins move their tails up and down to swim in the ocean.

NUTRITION

Living things need nutrients, or food, to live. Most living things eat the food they need. Plants make their own food by photosynthesis. They use sunlight to turn water and carbon dioxide into food. Plants use this food to live and grow. Some animals eat plants to help them live and grow!

Photosynthesis is the way plants use sunlight to make food.
Carbon dioxide is a gas found in the air.

Other animals eat the animals that eat plants. Zebras eat grass and then lions eat the zebras. Mice eat seeds and then foxes eat the mice. Cows eat grass and then people eat beef.

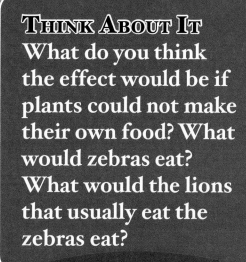

THINK ABOUT IT
What do you think the effect would be if plants could not make their own food? What would zebras eat? What would the lions that usually eat the zebras eat?

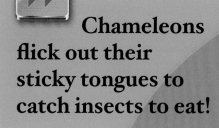

Chameleons flick out their sticky tongues to catch insects to eat!

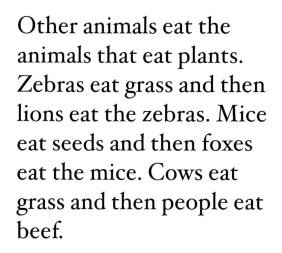

11

RESPIRATION

Food is useful to a living thing only when it releases energy. All living things need energy to grow, move, and carry out other life processes. Living things release energy from food by respiration.

Respiration happens throughout the body of a living thing when sugars from food combine with oxygen. Oxygen is a gas in the air. Many animals breathe in air through their mouths and noses.

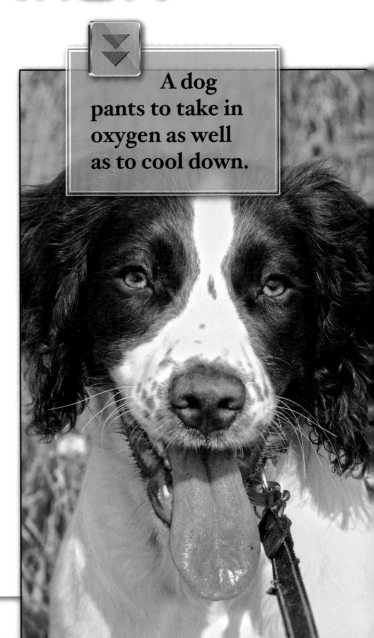

A dog pants to take in oxygen as well as to cool down.

Young newts take in oxygen from water through feathery gills on their necks.

Other living things get oxygen for respiration in different ways. Most plants take in oxygen from air through tiny holes, called stomata, on their leaves. Fish and newts take in oxygen from water using special body parts called gills.

COMPARE AND CONTRAST
People put fuel in a car to run the engine. How is food for humans like fuel for cars?

EXCRETION

Life processes create different types of waste. The waste can be harmful if it builds up inside living things. Excretion is the way the body gets rid of waste. During respiration, living things produce waste as a gas called carbon dioxide. Humans breathe out this gas from their mouths and noses.

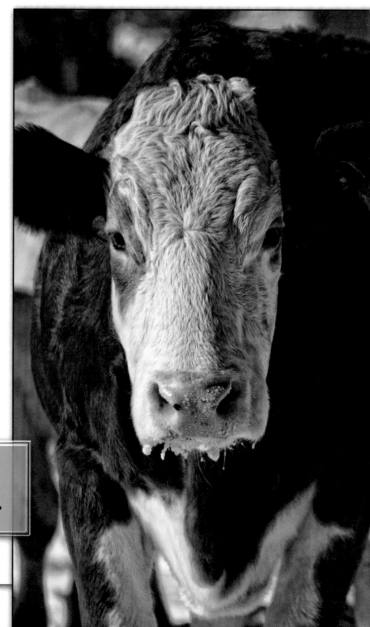

Animals breathe out carbon dioxide waste.

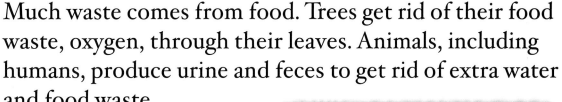

Much waste comes from food. Trees get rid of their food waste, oxygen, through their leaves. Animals, including humans, produce urine and feces to get rid of extra water and food waste.

The world would be covered in waste were it not for animals such as dung beetles. Dung beetles eat feces and lay their eggs inside it.

THINK ABOUT IT
Green plants use carbon dioxide waste from humans and animals to make food. Why might cutting down forests in which green plants live be a problem for our planet?

SENSES

Living things need senses to react to the world around them. Senses include touch, sight, hearing, smell, and taste. Animals use senses to find food and other animals to have young with, and also to escape danger. For example, a deer needs good hearing and eyesight to see an approaching tiger.

Owls hunt mostly at night. Their huge eyes help them spot animals, such as mice, in the dark.

THINK ABOUT IT

A fly's eyes are different from an eagle's. What parts do all eyes have in common?

Living things use different parts to sense the world around them. Tips of plant roots sense which way is down so that they grow into the soil. Catfish have whisker like feelers to find food.
A scorpion has tiny hairs on its pincers that feel air movements. This helps the scorpion to find prey.

Shoots sense light. They grow upward to reach it so they can make food.

REPRODUCTION

All living things reproduce—they produce new living things that look like themselves. Most plants reproduce by growing seeds from their flowers. When the seeds fall or blow away from the plant and land in dirt, they grow into a new plant. Some animals lay eggs and their babies develop inside the eggs until they are ready to hatch.

A bird egg has a hard shell to protect the chick inside the egg before it hatches.

Human babies grow inside their
mother for nine months before being born.

Mammals, such as lions, dogs, and humans, are animals
that have babies that develop inside the mother's body.
Marsupial mammals, such as kangaroos, have tiny babies
that must spend a long time in their mother's pouch
before they are able to survive in the outside world.

GROWTH

Living things grow by making new parts and materials and changing old ones. This happens when a seed grows into a plant or a chick grows into a hen. As humans grow, they add new parts, such as teeth, and change the size of others.

Trees keep on growing taller and wider every year.

A special kind of growth heals injuries. Shrubs and trees mend injuries by covering them with bark. Humans heal cut skin and mend broken bones.

Crabs grow new legs when old ones are lost.

STAYING ALIVE

Living things stay alive as long as they can carry out the life processes. If the life processes stop, they die. Some plants die if they do not get enough water or sunlight because then they cannot make the food they need. Animals such as lions may die if they are injured because they cannot move to catch prey.

Without water, plants cannot stay alive. They shrivel and die.

When living things are very old, they cannot carry out all of the life processes, so they die.

Life processes slow down and stop when living things reach the end of their natural life. As living things get old, the parts that help them grow, feed, move, and breathe start to wear out. Eventually, they stop living and die.

THINK ABOUT IT
All living things die, so what would happen if they could not reproduce? What would happen to living things?

GROUPS

Although living things have life processes in common, they can be very different. To help us understand and study living things, we can group them. We do this based on the similarities and differences in the ways living things carry out life processes, and by how many cells they are made up of.

Bacteria are single-celled living things. Some bacteria make us sick if they get inside our bodies and reproduce.

Cells are the basic building blocks of all living things.

One way to group living things is like this:

- Plants: make their own food by photosynthesis
- Animals: are made up of many cells and get energy they need from eating plants or other animals
- Fungi: can have one cell or many (such as mushrooms), but they are neither plants nor animals
- Microorganisms: are simple forms of life that can be as small as a single cell

NONLIVING THINGS

Nonliving things do not carry out the life processes. However, all nonliving things are not the same. Some things such as cars, cement, and metal were never alive. Others, such as wooden tables, hamburgers, and salad, were once living things.

This toy is a nonliving thing made from wood, which was taken from a living thing.

Coins are made from metal, which was never alive.

Nonliving things can be grouped into natural things and synthetic things. Natural materials include those that are dug out of the ground, such as rocks, or the metals that we get from rocks. Synthetic things are materials made in factories, such as polyester cloth and other plastics.

Synthetic describes something that is made by humans instead of taken directly from nature.

USING NONLIVING THINGS

A nonliving thing does not need anything to exist. It does not feed, grow, or reproduce because it is not alive. However, living things need nonliving things. We use some nonliving things to make our lives easier or simply for pleasure. People play games with balls and rackets, and we use machines to do work for us and to take us places.

We use some nonliving things to make life more fun!

We need some nonliving things, such as air and water, to survive.

We need some nonliving things to be able to carry out life processes. Plants need light and water to make food. Animals need plants to get the nutrition they need. Living things must have air to breathe to release energy from their food. Without these nonliving things, living things would not be alive!

> **COMPARE AND CONTRAST**
> Which nonliving things do people need to survive? Which do they need simply to make our lives easier or more interesting?

GLOSSARY

carbon dioxide A gas that plants use to make food, and animals give off when they breathe.

crystals Colorless rocks.

energy The power that can make things work, move, live, and grow.

excretion Waste from a living thing's body.

growth Getting bigger.

mammals Animals that give birth to live babies and feed their young on milk from their bodies.

marsupial A mammal that has a tiny baby that develops in a pouch on its mother's body.

movement Moving parts of the body.

nutrition To get nourishment from food.

oxygen A gas in the air around us. Oxygen is used for respiration.

pincers The claws of a scorpion.

polyester An artificial fiber made from coal and petroleum (oil) products.

prey Animals hunted for food.

reproduction To have young or babies.

respiration The act or process of breathing.

seeds The parts of a plant that produce another plant.

senses Smell, sight, touch, and other ways in which a living thing knows what happens around it.

similarities Qualities that things have in common.

survive To continue to live.

For More Information

Books

Claybourne, Anna. *Life Processes* (Raintree Freestyle: The Web of Life). North Mankato, MN: Raintree, 2012.

Hicks, Kelli. *Living or Nonliving?* (My Science Library). Vero Beach, FL: Rourke Publishing, 2011.

Kalman, Bobbie. *Is It a Living Thing?* (Introducing Living Things). New York, NY: Crabtree Publishing Company, 2007.

Rissman, Rebecca. *Is It Living or Nonliving?* (Living and Nonliving). North Mankato, MN: Heinmann-Raintree, 2013.

Living Things in Their Environment (Houghton Mifflin Science). Boston, MA: Houghton Mifflin, 2007.

Websites

Due to the changing nature of Internet links, Rosen Publishing has developed an online list of Websites related to the subject of this book. This site is updated regularly. Please use this link to access the list:

http://www.rosenlinks.com/lfo/liv

INDEX